DEDICATION

For me,

For the love
I long for most
Is my own.

WHERE THE HEART GOES TO BLOOM
Copyright Bloompress 2021

Writing is able to be shared via social platforms with the appropriate credit: @bloompress / Jessi Simpson.

All rights reserved. No part of this publication may be reproduced for any form or means, without prior permission from the author. This book is not permissible for re-sale / wholesale unless a direct agreement is made. For wholesale please contact via bloompress.com.au or visit hello@byjessi.com.

ISBN: 978-0-6450572-0-1

Finished design & words
by Jessi Simpson of Bloompress
@bloompress
www.bloompress.com.au

Cover Art:
Tahnee Kelland
@tahnee_kelland
www.tahneekelland.com

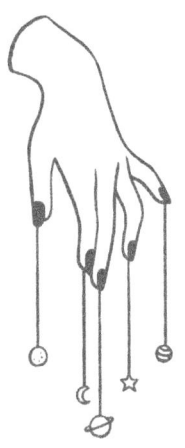

STARS FALL
FROM THE UNKNOWABLE,

-JUST AS WE DO.

She was created in the quiet of morning song,
Curled up in shapes written by my spine.
When my heart was still dreaming,
In a language only energy understands.

She found me, deep in the night sky,
In the landing-place of his steady heart,
So I could be shown what needed seeing.

She unveiled through the zesty flavours,
Of usual, everyday unfolding–
Where light danced me across old wooden floorboards.

Hiding in the shadows–
She followed me wherever the light lived.

The pages of her curvy, imperfect & raw body,
Calling upon me through morning kisses;
In a moonlight sway, in a pause to feel the coming day.

She percolated gently in rich black coffee
& crunchy peanut butter on toast–
Wrapping herself up somewhere in the middle
Of my falling apart & coming together again.

She is Love, with a capital L,
Despite it all.

WHERE THE HEART
GOES TO BLOOM

CONTENTS

INTRODUCTION　　xi

PHASE ONE
Fall　　1

PHASE TWO
Rise　　86

ACKNOWLEDGEMENTS　　203
ABOUT THE AUTHOR　　205

HOW TO USE THIS BOOK

Use with love,
Tuck yourself away
With a cup of something
You'd most prefer.
Read in order,
Or read with spontaneity.
Read these words
How you'd want to be undressed,
Each part of you–bit by bit,
Or with a fiery ferociousness.

& read knowing that you are made up
Of every archetype (the whole universe).
You are a single droplet,
Yet you are also the depths of the ocean.
We are all a unique expression of the universe,
& a part of the whole.

How do you want to be re-discovered?

INTRODUCTION

I undress to the sound of my breath now. I wrap my arms around the space-between, trying to grasp it all. At night, I tie my hair to the corners of the stars, swaying to the sound of being held by the sweetest of my sorrows, releasing to 70s song & aged wine.

The reason you & I are here together right now, interlaced between the words on these pages, is that this collection tapped me on the shoulder, wrapped itself around my knotted hair & moved me through a time–even before this–where we are all being called to meet ourselves in the colours we may have not yet had the courage to taste.

It doesn't really feel like it came from me, but from some sacred, untouchable energetic place that I have felt myself connected to in this season I find myself in. For me this is a true integration of the way I speak to the planets within Astrology, & the way they speak back to me.

She–this book–was always written in the stars. Perhaps she was the one who started whispering in my ear all those moons ago. This creation speaks in the language of soul, in the tongue of the Astrological archetypes, with a particular affixation with Pluto (the underworld.) I wrote it for myself, a soul who chose a Scorpio dominant incarnation. The rhythm & flow of these pages speaks to the waxing & waning of the Moon, the rising & falling of the tide & the two possible manifestations of an Astrological energy: light & dark. Mostly it speaks to the free-will inside of all of us, the part of us always in deep communion with the stars, the part of us that chooses the response. It's divine intervention meeting free-will.

She tells a story of effortlessness, acceptance, ease, even through navigating intensity. She has broken my own safety wall–this stubborn belief that if it's not hard, then I mustn't have tried hard enough. The cosmos doesn't respond to the silly demands of the mind. This book has changed it all. She was created lovingly, with no exact plan.

When I *tried* to birth her, she hid away under-covers, waiting for my heart & the dust to settle. Most importantly, to listen. Once life took my whole heart back again, & I was moved into a season of grief, anger, loss, uncertainty & change–every cell of my body knew that this was the time for this creation. & yet I knew that I still needed to leave enough room, and many-a-breadcrumb, to lead the words to *me*.

She's been waking me up at witching hour, tugging at my heart in the shower–chasing me, laughing!

& I have done my damnedest not to overthink this magical dance with the muse, but to close my eyes & feel, without making sense of any of it.

All so that you & I could unfold here, to release all we have held for so damn long, all that wasn't even ours to hold in the first place.

WHERE THE HEART
GOES TO BLOOM

The ending is the beginning.

How do you kiss goodbye?

WHERE THE HEART
GOES TO BLOOM

Phase One

FALL

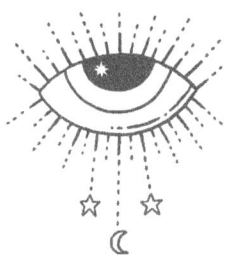

I am falling,
Away from everything,
I was planning, hoping,
Dreaming to become.

& I am finding a home crafted by,
Falling leaves, the cooling wind,
& a hands-in-the air surrender,
Of the parts of me that are no-longer.

In the falling away, I find a home.
A home that doesn't need anything from me,
Except whatever this moment calls in.

Making way for the kind of spaciousness,
I never knew I so deeply longed for.

EVAPORATING

One half of me–excited & full of all this new energy. The other half–broken & hurt, millions upon millions of pieces of me, sprawled out over the floor.

I am the endless rain. I am the cloudy sky, the flower that long ago rose to bloom. I am everything & nothing; giving birth, making room.

So many parts hold tight, the idea of us, one day again as lovers; suffocating, pushing down & away from the many parts aching to be set free, to soar the magic-hour sky.

Suddenly I feel a glimpse of warmth, emanating deep from the bones of me. I melt into the earth beneath, flashes of what has been shimmering through this rare glimpse of sunlight. The sorrow, the struggle–evaporating the surface of me.

It's been raining since you left.

THE STARS

He–music of sombre fire,
I–changing tides,
A chaotic hymn of romance & art.

My hair–messy again
After a wash the night before,
His fingers–lost again in tangles,
Knotted with ideas that fill
Entire rooms with potency.

& as we drive, he tells me;
This song reminds me of us,
"Baby, we set this whole thing on fire,
That time we came together again."

I hear the words down to my cells.
That we did, I muse.

Maybe we will see the stars again from here.

PLUTONIC

I'm wired intense,
Deep-written in my bones.

Today, I'm textured,
Rough around the edges.

Tomorrow, watch me awaken,
Soft, flowing.

I was created to burn up in feelings,
So I could get to their very end.

I was written in the stars to be a mystery,
Even to myself.

So don't ask me how I'm feeling,
Unless you really want to know.

There's no shallow water here,
I can only take you to the depths.

SPRING

When the flowers first bloom,
They whisper that I, too,
Have made it through a kind of darkness.

Springs first light, is a first breath anew,
An ode to all that is now blooming inside of me,
Transforming the dead, misplaced parts,
Into my own kind of beautiful symphony.

& like flowers, I find a home in the sun.
In the kind of steady, burning fire
That catches alight inside
& never stops burning.

WHERE THE HEART
GOES TO BLOOM

Close your eyes now,
Feel that?
The ocean's tide,
Setting within you.

—breath.

WHERE THE HEART
GOES TO BLOOM

My heart is the ocean,
My mind, as vast as the sky.

Part of it all.

WE COULD BE ANYWHERE

Words flow from mouths,
We wish we instead ate.

Reflections, dreams of a different tomorrow–
It is here, where my heart does nothing but ache.

My shadow, you are–mindless,
Drunk on life, cheap cigarettes & beer.

& that sunset, when we walked each other home
By the old train track, that summer night.

Tattooed city-walls, intoxicating evening air.
Street cats with piercing eyes;

We could be anywhere.

WHERE THE HEART
GOES TO BLOOM

LET LOVE RUN

The time has come,
Where being nice eats me alive.
& I feel each tear away at my flesh,
A whole chunk of me die,
Each time I tell the old story of you,
Believed once, not any longer.
Hear me howl at the top of my lungs–
The time has come, to let our love run
It's complex & intoxicated run:

Away.

MAGIC WE CAST

Never had I met anyone
Who–with palms to the sky,
& hearts to heavens
I could create bubbles of light with,
Where stardust speaks within
& the safest of expanded space.

Together we were this platform,
Delving deep into a darkness
That otherwise would have
Broken our bones,
Crumbled us to dust,
Consumed us whole.

& even when our conjoined
Worlds of beautiful chaos
Were slashed to part,
We still came together
One last time & drew from the well
We built from scratch,
Made of earth, ocean
Blood, wind & fire, so delicately strong.

WHERE THE HEART
GOES TO BLOOM

& we just sat there, one last time,
In this pure wonder of our little world,
With this ending,
We never thought would come.
Expanding silence so potent,
Knives could slice through it.

Just honouring the love
That decided to grace us
With one another
& the magic we had cast,
That would always live on.

–I love you, & goodbye.

WHERE THE HEART
GOES TO BLOOM

Bitter words never leave a sweet taste in their wake.

WHERE THE HEART
GOES TO BLOOM

A LOVE LIKE RICH SOIL

Can you love me,
Even if I am never whole again?
I whisper through shaken lips.

"Love is like rich soil,
Where entire fields of daisies
Grow from the old, discarded & smelly.

& oh the daisies I have seen bloom.
My love for you is no different.
I love you where life has broken you,
& I will love you when you bloom"

WHERE THE HEART
GOES TO BLOOM

New dawn, new day
Freshly bloomed roses, new sway.

WHERE THE HEART
GOES TO BLOOM

Turn my sadness into seeds.
Tears–watering them with prayer,
Bloom–the rarest of wildflowers.

–time.

THE WILLOW

You are a dream to me,
Except I close my eyes no longer
To dream your wonder.

Forever catching breaths,
When eyes click; floating,
Drifting in deep shades of blue.

Oceans meet the earth,
Blue is our warmest colour,
The colour of you.

Fun had, but not so–
That we were not in flow,
Completely.

Will you stop your strive,
& catch a breath in me?
When your eyes meet mine,

My curls are lit by your sundown rays.
Colours–seen, that will not stay.
In these rare shades, fairytales become true.

Perhaps just for me,
Perhaps just for you.
You think you are rolly,

But I think you to be
Like jumping in salty streams
When hot days flair.

& when I get home,
Hopes are always high,
For you being there.

Wrapping me up,
Just to unwrap me,
Fingers–ran through bodies.

WHERE THE HEART GOES TO BLOOM

Running my fingers through your hair
Sends me into the deepest of sleep.
We were ripened in the dark,

The taste of our tongues–
Always an aftermath of peanut butter
& coffee mornings.

Sleepless in ecstasy,
Night skies are gazing down on us.
Grazing on the willow above our heads.

Almost everything, blissfully out of grasp.

WHERE THE HEART
GOES TO BLOOM

How many different ways,
& in how many different shades
Of perfumed-colour,
Can you say "I love you"
To your own tender heart
Over & over & over again,
Before loves very essence–
All bright-eyed, timeless & wild,
Bursts right through it all?

What would it be like,
To rise, just as you are–here?

Right here where:
Sunflowers–bloom,
Dreams–rise to greet you,
Tears–set the seas,
& you–so radiantly you,
Already quietly,
Graciously–blooming.

COLOURS OF EARTH

Trappings & silhouettes of city noise,
Fold by fold–I lay between,
Two walls I mistook for my very home,
How long I lay here, I cannot know.

All I can know is,
I am far from the whispers
& my happiness is not
Where I thought it to be.

Skirts coloured with colours of earth,
A love to last a lifetime & days spent in grass,
Envisioning up a future of my brightest,
Will not send my breath reaching further.

Cell by cell by cell,
It's wrapped inside a darkness,
Behind two closed eyelids,
In the stillness of my body.

WHERE THE HEART
GOES TO BLOOM

Skin, fingers, heart–
Making up the edges of me.
Held trustingly by
The fleeting nature of this moment,

Where time stretches itself around just me.
My breath, & my heartbeat,
Until maybe one day,
I will be able to hear the whispers again.

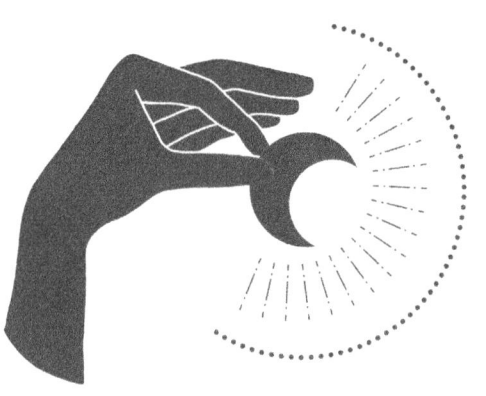

WHERE THE HEART
GOES TO BLOOM

Now is the season, to know that
Everything we do–is sacred.

WHERE THE HEART
GOES TO BLOOM

So, go on, allow the tears
To fill your heart up with gladness.

—letting go.

WHERE THE HEART
GOES TO BLOOM

ODE TO FREEDOM

History is a funny thing,
How she entangles us in her bittersweet repetition.

As one cycle becomes elongated,
The layers of existence seemingly deepening.

It reminds me of that feeling upon waking up
In the house I grew up in, thinking back to myself:

"How did I get back here?"
I circle back, again & again,

But now I have an entire life away from here,
Where new parts of me dance their brightest song.

& I am both the rose & the thorn,
All my parts mean so much to me now.

My bones, made of acceptance.
An ode to freedom.

WHERE THE HEART
GOES TO BLOOM

The pieces of my puzzle,
Remain all over the floor.
& I am still lost for words,
As you have them all.

−since you left.

WHERE THE HEART
GOES TO BLOOM

A once closed door,
Of everything we were & more—
Opened swiftly,
With one courageous sentence,
Sprawled out before us:
Our bright beginning:

—I'm going to kiss you now.

WHERE THE HEART
GOES TO BLOOM

My heart is the map,
The Sun is the melody.
I dance through my darkest hour,
For dawn–she longs to find me.

WHERE THE HEART
GOES TO BLOOM

My love, my love feels it all. There's no feeling, no nostalgic journey, no fiery sunrise my heart hasn't felt. Longing—for flower-tinged gifts, held by the one who shows up in bright-eyed knowing of the depths of me. Holding near—the sweet voice found when I know I am loved.

—moon-ruled heart.

AUTUMN SUN

How very sweet,
The things I have found,
When feet hit the ground,
To Autumn Sun's sound.

ROOM

Hold yourself, sit, be
Lean into it, fall away,
Unfold when the light
Finds a way through.

& when moon shadow drops,
Into your silent spaces,
Dancing all sweet sorrows,
Back to their never-ending places.

For your heart,
Longs to bloom,
Breathe in deep,
The magic to come–

Needs room.

WHERE THE HEART
GOES TO BLOOM

Under moonlit night,
Dreams seek me out, whispering–
Keep the light on so we can find you.

–*Neptune whispers.*

FERTILE SILENCE

We danced within the fertile silence. Grew within the soils of stillness, feeling into the unseen. All in a return to the blank-slate.

It is here, in this place of resounding nothingness, where we can drop down into the cool, rugged earth–deeper into ourselves. When we can stop & damn rest. Stop skimming the surface.

We go deep, like the roots of the oldest tree. For how can we create potently if we refuse this very important part of our creative process with life?

For what can truly be created, caught in the chains of burnout?

WHERE THE HEART
GOES TO BLOOM

& so the Rain & the Sun sat with one another, conspiring up a plan to help us grow within their delicate dance.

SILHOUETTE

The silhouette of my body is perfect art.
My fingertips, casting magic
With their tingling intention.

& every time I write his spine with my touch,
I imagine stars falling from the edges of me;
Whispering the tales of what it means,

To truly come home.

WHERE THE HEART
GOES TO BLOOM

You light up my night like the rising moon.

BROKEN SKIN

The door closes one last time on your already turned back. & I think you took half of my heart, & all of the sunshine with you.

As I struggle for clean breath, my hips can no longer bear my own weight. My knees become floorboards, & I imagine it morphing, Forming the perfect mould–soothing my broken skin.

I am pretending I am in the arms of the mother I have needed for so long. Body– furrowing deeper, reaching untouched dirt.

All I am is a naked weight, who forgot what the sun feels like.

WHEN MY SOUL
FALLS FOR YOUR SOUL-

SYNASTRY.

THE SWEET BETWEEN

It will come & it will go,
This much I know for sure.

Like the early morning hour,
Just before the dawn breaks.

Like the elongated pause between,
The deep inhale & expansive exhale.

The sweet between,
Where my soul felt

Something from your soul
& I was new again.

WHERE THE HEART GOES TO BLOOM

From one place,
There will always be
A longing for the other.

Hold tight to the top of your breath,
Where formlessness catches onto form,
& longs to be let go into nothingness.

Lovers don't finally meet,
Without having been
With each other all along.

WHERE THE HEART
GOES TO BLOOM

The morning after heartbreak,
Heart heavy, eyes swollen up
With the debris of the night before,
Screaming tears into sheets.

In front of me appears a rainbow,
Surrounded by dark storm clouds.
My heart swells as I think—

That's a brave rainbow, shining all bright.

WHERE THE HEART
GOES TO BLOOM

We both fall into a depth, un-returnable as we were. & we were always together, everything happens all at once, nothing inseparable. Today–created by yesterday. Tomorrow–made up of tiny today's & all the days before, without even existing yet. I want to breathe it all in, but I know time is not mine to know.

But it must be stretchy, as this very moment with you feels larger than all my days placed together.

You & I.

WHERE THE HEART
GOES TO BLOOM

Feel it all. Move from love.

WHERE THE HEART
GOES TO BLOOM

When things fall away & our hearts break over the line,
Of what was then & all we have dreamed up in our minds.
& we are on a tightrope with the universe both inside & out,
With no way of avoiding our own moments of falling.
In one way or another, whether it's in this place or the next,
Either way, it all ends with one deep, never-ending out-breath.

How can we continue to be in all of our now-moments?
& in the hands-shaking, heart-breaking, teeth-chattering moments,
Without looking away from ourselves?

When we can't possibly look pretty–here,
Or change what happened–here,
Or swallow those words spoken–here.

Here–at the top of loving bodies intertwined,
Between sips of rich wine,
& at the bottom of our final goodbye.

But then still loving & hurting so bad our bodies break,
& our eyes couldn't possibly shed another tear & yet they do.

& the unravelling into a million pieces for the part of us
That must leave now when life moves through.

ATTUNED

Don't resist the fall,
When it's the time to fall now.
There is a sweetness, a honey-soaked nectar
Awaiting you on the other side of the plunge.
& when it's time, that same sweetness
Will rise in you, become you.
& you'll feel yourself moved from this place.
Your edges, sharper than ever before,
Positioned to the world in a way,
That keeps the inside subtle, untouched.
Hungrier to drink the world,
Thirstier for the callings of your own heart.

LOVE & CIGARETTES

Swaying hips around the bend,
Of his heart & my oceans.
An invisible, magnetised cord,
Grounding up from the earth below.

The beat of the drum,
Jolts the fire in our bones,
Light beams through curtains,
Floating dust, unwashed sheets.

Full up on one another,
Yet empty of ourselves.
& while we drive,
We breathe in each other's smoke.

WHERE THE HEART
GOES TO BLOOM

Euphoric on love & cigarettes,
Or whatever this feeling is.
Floating–our bodies intertwine,
Wrapping each other up like a gift.

Running up deserted streets at midnight,
Stars–watching down.
& I think we are the moon,
Watching the stars
& the night sky right back.

Falling right back into each other,
Together–we lay, wanting forever.
But the alarm clocks creep up,
Running away from love again, to the day.

WHERE THE HEART
GOES TO BLOOM

What can I possibly do with all that I feel?
I write the Moon.
Just feel, Moon writes back.
Until morning Sun breaks.

Perhaps by then you'll have stopped trying to make sense of it all.

TAKEN BY STREET LIGHTS

Car headlights flare,
As the heavens
Pour down on us.

I take in the sheer sight of you–
Flanno, chiseled jaw.
Eyes–hungry as they search
For the meaning in
Your effortless words,
Floating out of your mouth
In cigarette smoke.

It feels like we could be
In an indie film,
Under this doorway
Looking up at the night–
Crying starless sky.

WHERE THE HEART
GOES TO BLOOM

You breathe your smoke
As we watch it rise, float, drift.
To be taken by streetlights.

& as we lower our gaze,
Tight jeans–sticking to bodies,
I feel my heart in my throat,
Hairs–standing all over.

& we breathe each other in,
Lips, uttering not a peep.
Eyes–telling love tales,
Told only in the most
Heart-stopping stories.

In this moment,
We have everything.

WILDFIRE

I miss the light, flickering off the burning fire of our love.
Like rich wine stoking embers, I caught ablaze in your slightest touch.

All started with a simple sunset walk, hearts–booming & sweet,
Quiet words–shared, carried by a gentle breeze & off into the night.

Catching onto ears, the entire galaxy–moved.
It was the beginning of a fire, that burned so bright,
That it couldn't help but consume us whole–quickly.

I miss the light, & those slow, long days in your loves burning embrace
–Sun, emanating as if from the very centre of us in togetherness.
Fully embodied, my curves–full with kisses & never lonely.

You loved as if we had an eternity of flickering flame,
A directional, sacred flow to downstream rivers with nowhere else to be.
You gifted me with it all, burned me up within your touch.

& as I was lit alight inside by you,
the space between what was & what was yet to be
Disappeared before my eyes. It was as if I could reach out
& touch time with my fingertips–change it all with
The alive flickering in my heart.

WHERE THE HEART
GOES TO BLOOM

I miss the light, flickering off this fire we created.
Words, pouring out into the centre of that burning blaze,
Sending me to depths I never dreamed to plunge into.

Love–with suddenly no place to go, as quickly as it caught alight,
It burned out & churned us up in it.

Where can love go now that you're gone?

Tears–catching onto the same wind
That held our first sweet conversation,
& I know the more I cry, the more I wash you & our wildfire, away.

WHERE THE HEART
GOES TO BLOOM

Who am I,
Wrapped up in the midst,
Of all this coming & going?

WHERE THE HEART
GOES TO BLOOM

What is real & true will stay,
Swaying us whilst we
Loosen our tight grip.
The rest will fall away.

BACK TO THE HEART

When all of a sudden, a stranger stops & smiles, I hope you feel what you thought was impossible to feel again–moving into the pit of your stomach. Like a ray of sunshine, making its way through the cracks of what broke you, I hope you know that in the falling apart, you are coming together in a way that words can't possibly explain.

Maybe the point is not to look pretty, or to always do 'good' or 'right' things. Maybe the point is to allow the ocean of life to move you to your own watery depths when life hurricanes in darkness & you can't possibly feel light–here. But what seeks to find you, seeks to find you–here. It's here–in the midnight tears & here–in the sweet early morning mull over coffee & first-light, where invitations back to your heart await you.

WHERE THE HEART
GOES TO BLOOM

Hands empty, heart full.

–love.

THE EVER UNRAVELING

Fingertips touch earth,
Rain falls on cheeks,
Dust seeps through air,
But breath still falters.

I let the traffic take me,
when I knew better.
I let the pain break me—
That unwritten letter.

Oh, to be alive & free,
Wandering with awe,
& to embace
The ever unraveling.

Life–unfolding.
Spontaneously intertwined,
Spirits, words, pain, bodies.

WHERE THE HEART
GOES TO BLOOM

The true teacher
Unfolds in nature.
Within every storm,
In my every breath.

We are nothing,
We know nothing,
& in that rawness,
A whole universe expands.

Of our own rhythm,
Of our own heartbeat,
Resisting time
Away from you.

MERCURY

& I just keep unraveling. Each word I write–freeing the old story. The veneers unwritten. Another part of me, stepping into light, roaming free under stars. Silent enough, to hear the whispering, the aching.

Walking free under the blue moon, drowning away the clothes I wear, to simply blend another facet, another untended to, unchained, messy part of me.

OOZING RED

I hear sounds
Of wind, birds, trees
Within the faintest corner
Of the setting day.

We are holding souls
In shaken hands,
Fingertips grasping
For words–unspoken.

Hearts swelling, bleeding.
We ooze red,
Over the damp green grass.

Bodies shaking, swelling up,
Inner worlds–
Screaming out for air.
Lips in slow motion.

WHERE THE HEART
GOES TO BLOOM

Carefully spilling words,
Slicing through the thinnest,
Most delicate air.

Stabbing straight through
Shattered souls,
& wishing achingly for just
One more day.

—last time I saw you.

WHERE THE HEART
GOES TO BLOOM

She is love,
Where love is
Least expected
To be found–

Venus.

WHERE THE HEART
GOES TO BLOOM

Can you direct your now
In the momentous rhythm
Of becoming & unbecoming
Yourself over & over,
Without holding tight
To good or bad
& right or wrong?

WHERE THE HEART
GOES TO BLOOM

Can you hear me?
Do you see me?
Are you fully here with me?

—arguments

THE OLD PIANO

Anew I am. All these stone walls got me feeling at home. Toes in sand, hand in hand, & that old piano. Where you'd always find me, in due season–when you'll come home again.

Your fingers can run away, from my hair, down my back. Home in the summer, when the sweat drips & we walk forever on the clouds. Away in winter, melancholic chill. Hot chocolate rarely spills. Just somewhere–

Caught in the corners of before & after.

VENUS, WOUNDED.

Everything is falling away & tears roll down my cheek. Heart–smashed into foggy glass mirrors. My head does cartwheels, on the road just driving.

Barriers between valves–broken. Giving up a fight–fought alone. Dragging dead weight across ever-moving finish lines. & placing my pieces, your way–in a hope that you would love them there.

Your shirt, I still wear. Now drenched in the water you slowly, but surely, noise-cancelled me within. Fragments of memory, by you so easily sunken. It's like I am forever forgotten, suddenly shipwrecked.

Like a shop closed for business, you turned out your lights the moment I very first fell for you, knees–bruising, swollen.

Like a stranger always searching, passing me by on an intoxicating city night–a vacant vessel, you were. I always hoped for a day where I would fall for you over again, & be caught.

WHERE THE HEART
GOES TO BLOOM

There is no win, there is no lose.
Just a void–heavy winds of change.

I gaze into the night, walking down backstreet alleyways & torn up concrete. Blazed upon with non-stop rains, feet–forever chasing time away–consuming it all up in quick-minutes & black coffee.

I'm scared that if I stop my forever-run from silence that the backdoors will unlock & the slow black mornings will return to me again. Mirror reflections: grieving, shedding, falling apart & slowly-turning toward all I can be when I am not skimming the surface.

Laced textures intertwining our limbs, colliding worlds & words each night as heads hit pillows. & I am floating, in oceans of a life with you, swimming strokes I know I won't dare swim forever. Tides, so steady–twirling in our final midnight-hour together as sweet lovers.

You see, loving is a delicate thing, all wrapped up in the deepest of layers, velvet-drenched mornings & intoxicated alleyway nights.

Him–the cosmic mirror to my brightest undoings.

WHERE THE HEART
GOES TO BLOOM

My mind, how she sways like fierce winds. She dances up the sweetest tunes, sways to songs of deep longing for all that holds no form.

Until I realise that I have forgotten for a moment how it feels when you're gone, & I catch my soul whispering–

Take me back to that place, the place I was, before I found myself broken.

The breeze, settling with my breath.

WHERE THE HEART
GOES TO BLOOM

Your blood is the ocean,
Capable of a wildness that kills,
A churning depth that transforms,
& a stillness that can't help
But feel wild in some sacred way.

For you, there is always more–
More to be felt, more to be tasted.
& the world longs to be knocked to its knees,
To meet you in this deep resounding depth–

Archetypal Scorpio Wisdom.

WHERE THE HEART
GOES TO BLOOM

There is no distance between you & your heart–

Messages from the moon in Sagittarius.

WHERE THE HEART
GOES TO BLOOM

Simply show up.
Slowly, silently–move.

Saturn Integrity.

Oh, how you care with that heart made of refined gold. How can one be loved by you & not be moved further toward themselves? I will never know—

Capricorn energy.

WHERE THE HEART
GOES TO BLOOM

No other place exists–

Here.

Your midnight star-gazing & fierce way—a daily revolution for all that walk the path with you. Your love is all encompassing. Your heart is the new way—

Aquarius Moon.

WHERE THE HEART
GOES TO BLOOM

A direct transmission of soul, you–the background longing deep within the hearts of many–

Inner Pisces.

WHERE THE HEART GOES TO BLOOM

Where do you long to be understood in a love language many have not yet discovered?

Step forward–here. You don't need to be understood to move from this place. You are the sun, illuminating the world for the very first time.

Aquarius energy.

WHERE THE HEART
GOES TO BLOOM

The out-breath *(the sweet letting go)*
Unveils the first step.

WHERE THE HEART GOES TO BLOOM

Forget the nice, well behaved girl,
Leave her at home.

Choose the wild midnight calling,
Rattling in your bones–

Initiation.

Phase Two

RISE

You'll find me among the banks of dawn.

I am the one with the burning fire in the pit of my stomach. My feet, aching to dance to a song that has not yet been sung.

I am the one whose dreams catch effortlessly onto each changing wind. I have woken up where romance & inspiration bloom, like flowers opening to early morning sun.

I am the one with the ignition spark, to all that is wild, rebellious & true.

To rediscover me, first rediscover you.

WHERE THE HEART
GOES TO BLOOM

Leave the words
To float amongst themselves.
As this love is one,
That cannot be explained.

WHERE THE HEART
GOES TO BLOOM

Life–never as sweet when I
try to dance it all on my own.

NEPTUNE JOURNEY

I set the space. The palo santo burns, waving down the heavens. Each moment unfolds & it's as if the walls become soft with cushioning for my body. Each choice of what gets invited in to the only thing that ever exists–the here, now–made with a precision & decisiveness I have never before felt.

I start to understand the agonising frustration–my own inward build-up–of what I have not yet grasped. I feel myself, floating on this magical edge. This edge, where the intensity is so wide, full-bodied, & explosive, just before the page is turned toward the chapter of breakthrough.

I have been pulled, poked & pushed to capacity. I have been thrown around by my own insatiable need to always be in a meeting of the outer. But I know, from the deepest knowing place, that I am in the final throes & throbbing pain of a metamorphosis.

The build up of the rain pouring outside the window–still held by clouds. I've simply been holding, retaining, meeting with the intensity of the grief that doesn't always go so easily processed, when caught in the thrashing chains of humanness.

●

Suddenly, it feels like I have always known what to do. My breath-out reaches a place where I swear the entire beat of the universe moves from. & what I have been running from is this fear that if I enjoy being in this place–inside of myself–for too long perhaps I will no longer be myself. I will no longer have anything to hold onto, I will no longer want to be in the world.

But in this sweet meeting, the whisper of sweet, divine timing places her hand to my spine & tells me–*you do not need to fret now, you are ready.*

PRACTICE–

Inhaling–
My hands move the up length of my body as I invite the heavens down into my crown, through my body, into my feet. Roots begin to grow from my soles.

Retaining–
Thinking mind, dissolving. The flowers can begin their bloom.

Exhaling–
I draw my hands back down my body, tuning into my palms. My chin lifts spontaneously, that subtle tingling. Drawing energy up the spine, back out into the universe.

Retaining–
I am being breathed out. I don't have to try to do the breathing any more.

It's me who is truly being breathed. This body–breathed & lit up by consciousness. The clouds drop their first drop of rain. & another, followed by another. In this sweet, courageous allowing, I feel breath reaching, showing me the way.

I drop it all; anything I know about movement, anything I know about breath-work, anything I know about meditation, anything I know about anything at all. Because who am I to know? It's not up to me to know it all on the level of the mind. I am simply here to feel, to experience, to be moved, to co-create. It's funny to think in this moment how I could have ever expected myself to know as much as I thought I needed to know.

There is an undercurrent, connecting each motion, each sigh, each release, each inclination, each conscious thought. & then somewhere, in the middle of a breath, clouds began to release, their pour–the heavens dropping down on me.

I know it's time to take the journey. I plant intentions so deep that I am so very held within. I take myself to the doorway, where the breeze holds a sweet tang.

& I take a seat, only just sheltered enough from the rain, that I can still feel it's kiss. I hear the sounds of night. With each draw-in of the sacred smoke, the edges between me & this night dissolve. I move my body further out into the rain, trusting in this night, being the one I take the journey. I watch the smoke, merging upward into cloudy skies.

I go to do something, thinking that I can make it back before I am called, but something pulls me to sit back down.

I feel my lowest energy centre heating first. Turning up the dials rapidly, my ears hum–the edges of my body, dissolving quickly. I sit myself in meditation, posturing my spine straight up toward the cosmos as this heating, this cosmic vibration, slowly floods out through my entire body.

I am sent out-of-body. I have no body. All I feel is a calm, steady ringing & buzzing. The harmonium sings louder & I feel myself as vibrational existence. Everything is black, except for this grid of stars lighting up the night like thousands of exploding moons.

I am hovering far above the Earth, somewhere in the centre of it all. I feel the movement of my energy, the heat & buzzing, rapidly surging upward & out the top of my head. The more I sit still, the more I very quickly feel myself plunging, letting go, losing attachment to the physical feeling of 'me.'

I am surging light. I am a dancing sky in another galaxy. It is so beautiful, tears well. Is this what death feels like? The body is the only thing that gets old. How nice it is to feel the weight of the body, dropping. Perhaps this is what it feels like to just be a cluster of vibration, of light, in connection to it all–so sweet. But we humans can only hold to form, to what we know.

I feel as if I want to tell everyone how beautiful this is, everyone I leave behind. They don't need to cry over me one bit. I am everything, I am everywhere, I am free.

I feel pangs in my stomach, my body telling me I am still here. & it feels like I am pulled back by fear, fear of not being able to be in my body. Not being able to have the touch of my lover. His kiss. The very real feeling of sunlight on skin, & the delicious feeling of my taste buds.

I am back down for a moment & I see him walk past. Back within this room, I am guarded & protected. I am safe. This existence I am living, this incarnation, feeling significant. I get this feeling my soul has been waiting for this, this deep remembering.

Suddenly I feel myself rocking back and forth, wrapped up in this sweet, slow dance. It's a dance, a rhythm I have felt glimpses of before but never fully understood.

WHERE THE HEART GOES TO BLOOM

I feel the back of my head heat up like sun, accompanied by a nudge in the back of my heart, a sharp pinching, a buildup. I lean back into it, & I am held up completely. I am suspended in space. Linear time, non-existent. This rocking back & forth becomes a whole spinal wave, followed by a wave of the whole body.

This slow motion, this rhythm, breathing me in & shooting me out every single round. I am overcome, by a deep churning in the heart. A chain reaction of warmth, of circulating particles, being set off–finally able to move their way. I notice the water flowing in through my lips, down into my ears. It's as if the storm outside is flowing from my eyes.

It is here, in this ecstatic joy, where my heart drops what feels like a lifetime of turmoil, of holding, of fretting, of taking on what is not mine, of the gravity of the world. I am floating in a slip-stream, a deep undercurrent of blue-tinged motion, expanding, expanding. With each sway, breath, pulse, the motion naturally becomes bigger, expanding–spontaneously. My whole body is simply being moved, without moving one muscle.

In this stillness, in this silent breath—where the soul lives.

WHERE THE HEART
GOES TO BLOOM

The closest I've come to perfection–when I look inward.

STAR-SEEDS

Our hearts are star-seeds, burning up for each other.
& whatever is here–now–all that we have,
Either way it all ends, with one earth-shaking high,
& the two of us, wrapped in velvet-tinged feeling,
Surrendering the need for more, curling inward.

HOME AGAIN

Sun-beams, bright lights, afternoon kisses,
& I am home again.

Home again–in birdsong outside my window,
Home again–softening into his chest,
Beating with roses-to-bloom
& telling old stories of alleyway nights,
Smoking cigarettes to your favourite reggae tune.

Home again–in the simple bliss between fresh linen sheets
& tomorrows that speak of freshly cut flowers.
Home again–in cold black coffee,
As my heart catches in a dream that truly takes me somewhere.

Home again–whenever I choose to be.

WHERE THE HEART
GOES TO BLOOM

Feel that subtle tingling
In the palm of your hands?

The wisdom of the planets,
speaking to you.

WHERE THE HEART
GOES TO BLOOM

Going to my own depths,
Makes me more in the world
Than those caught in the chase,
Of its impermanent trappings.

Choosing to trust in my heart.

WHERE THE HEART
GOES TO BLOOM

To own my own experience of it all

—the greatest gift I could ever offer.

WHERE THE HEART
GOES TO BLOOM

I feel myself falling away
From all I was hoping,
Dreaming, planning to be.
& landing exactly where I am.

& if only I could explain,
Just how sweet that feels.

My bones–made of forgiveness,
Heart–filled to the brim with grace.

–my ode to freedom.

WHERE THE HEART
GOES TO BLOOM

Space to fly & feel the roses grow. Places that help us feel, & breathe & learn things all on our own. Not too early, not too late, she'll be there knocking at the door to my heart & home, hands-full of coffee, flowers & cuddle offerings, reminding me that, we aren't meant to do it all alone.

WHERE THE HEART
GOES TO BLOOM

I know I've been quiet. But if you have been looking for me, you'll find me here—within this place where breath flows & the heart comes to let go.

GATHER

How invigorating not needing to understand really is.
When bodies, energies & intentions,
Fill a space with delight & prayer.

& with this gathering,
We can't help but re-learn,
How to be with ourselves.

At the dawning of a new day,
We dance to wisdom's silent sound,
A courageous, outward sway.

Filled with a room of strangers,
Wrapped up together in this space-between,
Open completely to an emptiness, unseen.

Permeating out, this wholeness so endlessly giving.
Diving into our out-breaths,
Together–dancing a rhythm

Our hearts have been searching for so long to find.

Have you ever experienced something so profound with someone you had never even met before that very moment? What did you do with that? I guess only the heart can really know.

WHERE THE HEART
GOES TO BLOOM

How magical is it when
You let everything go
& it's like the earth whispers
"I've got you"

—held, always.

WHERE THE HEART
GOES TO BLOOM

He is like sun,
Warming & evaporating my surfaces.
With each touch of his light,
I am elated by his long-awaited morning,
Challenged by the burning up of midday.

& I am the moon,
Churning up his tides,
Moving things where they need moving,
& surrendering thought over,
In the name of the unknown.

–polarity.

SURRENDER

How I long for the deep exhale,
That sweet release of the weight,
Of all I have been through–
The entire universe, breathing me out.

I feel the hands of creation,
Longing to draw art upon my spine.
Weaving delight through my breath,
Surrendering the need to be okay.

I want to fall asleep loving you.

—one of the sweetest thoughts, I ever did have.

WHERE THE HEART
GOES TO BLOOM

I still may not have
Much of a clue,
About loving you at all.

But this *(places hands on heart)*
–this I know.

WHERE THE HEART
GOES TO BLOOM

Falling into arms that feel new each night,

–a love that has a life of its own.

WHERE THE HEART
GOES TO BLOOM

Plant seeds & dreams,
Wish upon a star,
Then, when the dreaming is done–play.

The true rebellion.

WHERE THE HEART
GOES TO BLOOM

I long to spend more afternoons,
Wrapped in sunshine, words
& our mis-matched bed sheets,
Flooded with loving you.

WHERE THE HEART GOES TO BLOOM

It's dancing around the house, rearranging art in new places. It's hearing a song singing one moment, blooming flowers in my mind & needing to dance to it so loud until I know for sure, I have been danced by something greater. & it's the need for complete silence & wide-open nothingness in the very next. It's sneaking an extra 5 morning kiss moments, wrapped up in readiness. It's rolling out my yoga mat on the back veranda, just in time for the afternoon sun to hit. It's falling asleep to movies & back scratches. It's the sunset sky. It's that first sip of wine, that first hello after far-too-long. It's foraging for wildflowers in faraway places (my backyard counts). It's listening–really listening–without the need to say anything at all to fix it. It's floating in the ocean, feeling like a beautiful spec amongst it all– being moved. It's my ear to your chest–creations thump. It's closing my eyes & meditating on nothing in particular, to then remember how much I wanted avocado toast this morning–right before these words swiftly caught me in the breeze. It's the sunshine, making her way through sea-stained windows. It's black coffee in bed on a Sunday afternoon, catching his gaze between the pages of an old poetry book. It's knowing that deep rest opens magical doorways. It's you, looking at me the way you do–

Where I find my breath again.

WHERE THE HEART GOES TO BLOOM

The silhouette of my body is perfect art.
My fingertips cast magic with tingling intention.
& every time I write his spine with my touch,
I imagine stars falling from my fingertips,
Whispering tales of what it means to truly come home.

DUST

Perhaps it's not too good to be true–the contentment I am feeling in breathing the deepest, heartiest breath I've felt hit my lungs in the longest of whiles.

Your warm hands, finding my waist between covers each morning–the same hands that catch my midnight tears.

Perhaps it's not too good to be true, this freedom to move to my heart's extravagant, wild beat; adjusting my pace to slow, & on whatever makes the heart let-go.

Perhaps it's not too good to be true; nestling into you for 1000 sundowns & more. Many nights–spent in Brunswick Street alleyways, listening to your favourite tune. Belonging to those moments together, reverently with each step, sway, boogie, twirl–electric kiss.

Losing our way–to find it wherever life has moved us. Perhaps it's not too good to be true, finding this sweet love as the world crumbles to dust–

You, me–us.

WHERE THE HEART
GOES TO BLOOM

& like flowers, I find a home in the sun.

Does it ever leave—
This wanting you?

I hope not.

How wild it is, when suddenly I realise I am looking up & I cannot remember the last time I truly did.

—*listening, again.*

WHERE THE HEART GOES TO BLOOM

Your heart is Moon-ruled.
A doorway made of ocean tides,

Worth sitting in the Sun all day
To listen intently to.

—are you listening?

WHERE THE HEART
GOES TO BLOOM

When I am with you,
I feel how flowers must feel
When they are kissed by sunshine.

WHERE THE HEART
GOES TO BLOOM

I want to drink the world.

–says the unstoppable, Gemini heart.

WHERE THE HEART
GOES TO BLOOM

BREATHE OUR OWN BREATH

Away from you, there is no longing. Just a deep inward turning, to sit quietly & watch the rise & fall of my breath. I used to long for you, I still do. But now this longing is supported by the foundations we have built–this irreplaceable freedom to breathe our own breath.

This natural rhythmic ebb & flow, this intuitive drawing inward to reacquaint myself with all that is wild, all that longs to find me behind closed eyes.

I draw the blinds to a close in my hotel room, dust–floating through light beams. The chasing vibration of city noise–a welcome hum to my ears.

My delightful, playful invitation to let it be, to go my own way–for now. Each motion, each movement; like a thought, a passer by in a never ending dance so much bigger than me.

WHERE THE HEART
GOES TO BLOOM

A folding inward, the heartbeat of something new. Something untouchable, unseeable, but felt: like nothing I have ever felt before.

Like a river, love flows, becoming me with it's momentous sway. Try to grasp it & it slips through fingertips.

Oh how I long to dance with all that longs to dance with me–as form longs for formlessness, & the moon in the night sky longs for midday sun.

I smell your scent on a shirt of yours, snuck away with me as I left. & I am catapulted into a starry sky filled with you. I didn't wait for this feeling. & yet here it is, slow dancing me to lay it down.

Sun weaves in & out of the clouds, I am home in both the longing & the knowing.

WHERE THE HEART
GOES TO BLOOM

These are the days I wished a star upon.

WHERE THE HEART
GOES TO BLOOM

One day we'll go slow enough,
To watch the Sun rise from our own bed.

WHERE THE HEART
GOES TO BLOOM

I believe the morning air,
Holds secrets–dancing
& whispering the tales of magic,
Meant for me, into the curls of my hair.

WHERE THE HEART
GOES TO BLOOM

She is a wild calling,
A 12am howl.
The inconvenient & the thrilling,
Spanning the depths of the ocean,

—muse.

WHERE THE HEART
GOES TO BLOOM

Sacred words—free to roam
With heart & adventurous tongue

Everything feels random on the surface
With each little moment—carried out
Through radical heartbeats & winds of
Change leading to everywhere & no where.

—*age of Aquarius.*

WHERE THE HEART
GOES TO BLOOM

WHAT DRAWS US NEAR

Sipping on depth & texture,
In shades of red stomach's–
Churning up on love & the music
Rain leaves on concrete,
On summer evenings,
Where the air is so thick
You can almost taste it.
& a fire burns in our hearts,
For what draws us near.

WHISPERS OF HOME

It feels like only yesterday, when my whole being, my every thought, my every choice was moving me irrevocably toward my now.

Only very few footsteps from our favourite local (& oh how there are many). Sunrises spent with toes in sand, warm cups of love in one hand & his in the other.

Oh the whispers of days ahead I have felt, dancing through messy untamed hair, speaking of little miracles that I long ago braced my heart for.

In this little place, where the mountains kiss the sea.

WHERE THE HEART GOES TO BLOOM

I rise early to feel the quiet calling of morning-sun.
Stepping out of the way, even from my own wants.
Being moved through finely-shaped doorways,
Elevating through a delicate stream of consciousness,
Each deep breath, a rebellious act,
A soulful sabbatical in & of itself.

–Surya Namaskara.

WHERE THE HEART
GOES TO BLOOM

& the more time goes on & on
The more it is written in the divine fabric,

–I was made for loving you.

WHERE THE HEART
GOES TO BLOOM

The details will always loom,
Screaming in corners.
But there's this river,
It flows so powerfully,
Running straight through
The centre of it all.
All worry, all fear,
All impatience, all control.
It blasts its own fierce direction,
Straight to the heart.
& it's here I realise,
As I let the river
Absorb me to the bone,
That the details were never really mine
To tend to in the first place.

WHERE THE HEART
GOES TO BLOOM

Oh, the loving that we've learned,
Is going to keep us breathing.

EMPTINESS

I remember the moment I found you, like stumbling upon accidental treasure within the crashing waves, within beach-afternoons. It was the first time my whole body spoke of wanting someone, without my mind stubbornly needing to 'make it be so.' What a strange feeling indeed, to see you for the first time & feel myself emptied.

This emptiness, so beautiful that tears would well & the Sun suddenly wants to rise again. This—the kind of emptiness that obliterates & creates everything that exists & thrives.

You walked into my room that night, & just like that, we watched as our whole lives before that very moment rattled to the ground without even trying. The whispers in our hearts, shook the ground & tore away the comfortable veil of friendship, nestled between us.

Bodies—trembling with magic. Realising the keys to our entire souls, breathing each other all along.

WHERE THE HEART
GOES TO BLOOM

For the seasons, they long to dance within my hair.
To lay their sweet, varying kiss upon my cheek.
& to hold me in falling Autumn leaves,
For the calling of all that longs to find me–

Heard only in the silence.

WHERE THE HEART
GOES TO BLOOM

Wild things happen in the steadiness of this love. In the walls of our home, in beginning's dust & gritty 2am conversation. In simply falling asleep at 8pm, back to back–in the sharing of dreams, with such wildness, simply because they are shared. Don't you feel it, within this sharing, the feeling expanding? In his fingertips, reaching for my hips. Our love always brews, like rich coffee–

In the stillness of morning.

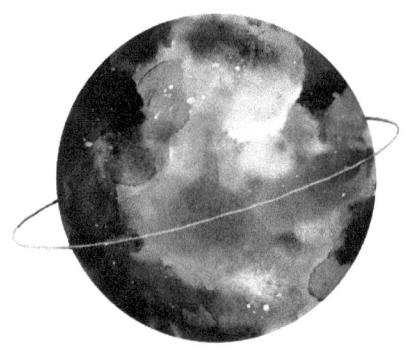

WHERE THE HEART GOES TO BLOOM

A constant ebb & flow
Between open conversations,
& sweet silence—
Intimacy & spaciousness:
The recipe for a magical love.

Holding space & being held.

WHERE THE HEART
GOES TO BLOOM

You & the moon are the sweetest of lovers, lighting up each dark night with your piercing gaze–

Taurus.

VENUS

Watering flowers to bloom,
A skin to Earth delight.

Undressing at dusk,
Swaying into the night.

To climb under-covers,
Here & now, it's all alright.

Oh, the revelations to be found,
In rich wine's bite.

WHERE THE HEART GOES TO BLOOM

Every new thought, planting entire worlds. Your mind, blooms like a wildflower. You are winds of change, acting upon every calling, every idea & impulse.

You are the muse, when she calls & the one who answers the call, all in the one. You are golden gifts, in the form of bold love notes–a strip tease of minds, dancing the same silhouette.

Love to you says: *you are free because I free myself every damn moment–*

Gemini's sweet melody.

WHERE THE HEART
GOES TO BLOOM

How often do you turn up the dials, on your connection to what moves you? Increase the sound of that wild heart, go on, I dare you. Oh, the flowers that bloom here in the potent humming of stillness. Water the feeling that calls you here; allow that wholeness to flock to you.

WHERE THE HEART GOES TO BLOOM

It's unfolding, into the painted lines that both paint me alive in rich colour & unravel me undone. This sunset place, with the laughing kookaburras & painted red skies, as Sun bows to Moon. Here, a moment opening into infinity—

Contentment.

WHERE THE HEART
GOES TO BLOOM

Can you see it up there, our big love, painting itself across night skies In crimson red?

WHERE THE HEART
GOES TO BLOOM

A leap too bold for the many, for you—a delightful, playful invitation, leading expansively into wide open spaces.

—*Sagittarius.*

WHERE THE HEART
GOES TO BLOOM

JUPITER'S KISS

Adventure awaits–you are the
breath that takes us there.

'Oh, you are so beautiful & you shine so bright!' Says Moon.

'I know, aren't I spectacular?' Replies Sun.

—the Leo spark.

WHERE THE HEART
GOES TO BLOOM

Wildest dreams hide somewhere between *nothing makes sense yet* & *everything is always falling into place.*

WHERE THE HEART GOES TO BLOOM

The sun, the moon & the oceans
They shine from your eyes.
Oh, how they have stories to tell
On love & trust & falling apart—
Finding wholeness over & over.
From the wildest of lineages,
Catching your bright gaze.
You gifted me the deepest breath
I have breathed in a long time.

WHERE THE HEART GOES TO BLOOM

You've shown me the beat of slow, the bold meaning of steady. Through lively banter, created by simple todays that say–

I'm not sure where I'm going,
But boy I'm having fun right here.

A Taurus love.

WHERE THE HEART GOES TO BLOOM

How did I get here?
How did it come to this?
I awaken, wrapped up within
The deepest teachings on rest I've ever felt,
Playing with the heartiest breath I've ever known–

Questions I place on the wind as the world tumbles down.

WHERE THE HEART
GOES TO BLOOM

I lean into the corners of my desire,
Re-igniting these flavours of me,
Long-ago faded.
I curl up in the static aliveness
Of city streets & intoxicated nights,
Intertwined between
My own sharp edges & watery softness,
Marinating my bones
In all that I already am.

–worshipping my urges.

WHERE THE HEART
GOES TO BLOOM

Sexuality is your own canvas,
To be explored & crafted upon.
So don't let the world
Catch on to your paintbrush
& turn what was always apart of you
Into a stranger.

Black Moon Resonance.

WHERE THE HEART GOES TO BLOOM

Growth may look like traveling backwards on the surface.

We are being called now, to access the deepest level of our being.
We are being invited now, into a reinvigoration & realisation,
That the same vibration that exists inside of us,
Also hums the potent tune of all that co-exists,
Emanates out, fluctuates & breathes back into the universe.

We are being breathed now,
By the deep, enlivened breath of all we already are.
We are being transformed now, aching to access the quiet
& darkened stillness flowers must feel–

Right before they bloom.

WHERE THE HEART
GOES TO BLOOM

Take me out of my depth,
Make me tread in your waters.
Give me a taste of my own medicine,
Tracing magic into my nerves.
Move me down to my bones,
In ways I can't move on my own.
& do that thing where
You wipe me of all I know,
To show me all I already am.

—Black Moon Lilith Cycle.

WHERE THE HEART
GOES TO BLOOM

You are a brightened morning,
The glimmer of creative spark,
Approaching us at midday–
A wild communion of life.

You are the electricity hidden,
Within every moon rise–
Always leaving breathing room,
For all that has not yet been created.

Your love language lives,
Where creativity & generosity do.
The sacred fire burns,
Within your open-hearted play.

Each footstep left behind,
A wildflower blooms.
Alive in your electric spirit,
Heart–made of pure sun-rays.

–ruled by the sun.

WHERE THE HEART
GOES TO BLOOM

Life loves in full vitality,
Wherever you are.

Leo.

WHERE THE HEART
GOES TO BLOOM

This part of you, for feet to land & hearts to grow. This part of you, that always knows. This part of you, where the physical body blooms toward the way forward.

–embodied Virgo wisdom.

WHERE THE HEART
GOES TO BLOOM

Discovering beauty & perfection where others don't even dare to glance–

Channeling the Virgo within us all.

You are the sweet reminder of the greatest story ever told. One of fully communing with each full belly breath. Each practice, each offering. There is purposeful music to be found in your love that knows no end.

—Mercury's breath.

WHERE THE HEART
GOES TO BLOOM

A sacred love is not seperate from everyday unfolding.

WHERE THE HEART
GOES TO BLOOM

Lending ears so peacefully, prompting hearts to bloom.

–Libra energy.

WHERE THE HEART
GOES TO BLOOM

The gentle, outlasts the strong.

LIBRA

Anything your heart catches on the wind, can't help but become beautiful.

I want you to know that simply being in your presence is enough for others to know they belong–

Messages from the Moon in Libra.

WHERE THE HEART
GOES TO BLOOM

Love is not an emotion. It's our very existence.

WHERE THE HEART GOES TO BLOOM

May you create sp a c e
Each morning,
To sit & sway.
With your brightest unknowns–

You are sacred.

A LOVE MADE OF SUNDAY MORNINGS

Morning–an act of togetherness.
Sun–streaming down, lighting up the dark spots.
Coffee–our love growing with every sip.
Eyes–on you.
Walking–slowly down memory lane, your fingers tip-toeing down my spine as you retrace our great, paradoxical love.
Covers–rolled, crinkled, unkept.
Avocado–the dreams of the day awaiting us.
Home–where we chose to courageously arrive together.

A song, drifting through the confines of linear space & reality, always to get to the essence.

Pisces wisdom.

If feelings were a language,
how would you speak?

Without words.

WHERE DANCING IS MORE COLOURFUL

Out in the ocean,
Where the waves churn
& go their own way,
I'll meet you there.

Deep in the valley,
Covered with wildflowers,
Bees, & floating leaves
Where there are no lines,
For right or wrong,
I'll meet you there.

Out in the rain,
Where dancing is more colourful,
& steps are full of new texture,
I'll meet you there.

WHERE THE HEART GOES TO BLOOM

In the space-between,
The rise & fall,
The holding & the surrender,
I'll meet you there.

In the falling of eyelids,
At each sundown,
Where anything is possible,
I'll meet you there.

WHERE THE HEART
GOES TO BLOOM

The Aquarius love is one that teaches the world to more reverently sit with itself.

WHERE THE HEART GOES TO BLOOM

The part of you that would risk it all, over & over again, if you knew a sweet surrender awaited you on the other side–

Jupiter's expansion.

CURVES

Every single curve on my body—
Kissed each morning.
My curves grow, then shrink.
The tide comes in & does not stay.
Because nothing is ever as it was,
& the same is nothing really at all.

EVERY LAST LINE

Intertwined between salty locks,
Twisty hair, thorns of the rose,
Sprawled between my legs.
Fingertips running away,
Down your back, lips–
Breathless, busy.
Tracing every last line,
Dancing with this pure joy,
Spirits turning over,
Bodies–so delicate.
Always catching up,
& my head spins–

Invigoratingly, in love with you.

WHERE THE HEART
GOES TO BLOOM

BEFORE COMING DAWN

Traffic gets wonderfully busy,
Outside our nook.
Brick walls, fairy lights
Unwashed crinkled sheets.

We are a mystery, under covers.
Skin on skin, hips teasing.
& those three, heart stopping words,
Dancing around in our heads.

Ocean blue eyes piercing,
Through my soul.
That held breath,
Your gaze on my breast,
That pure wonder.

Before coming dawn,
Over endless waters,
We fall on our sides
Not quite knowing
For just how long we've
Stretched out each other's body.

Tides within me rise & fall,
& I just watch.

WHERE THE HEART
GOES TO BLOOM

UNVEILING

I love the smell of smoke in dusk air,
When the cold stabs at my core.
& I can see words in my breath.
I imagine you & I around a fire,
Kissing under light of a full moon.
Firing up your eyes,
Crystallising our love through entire
bodies–trembling with magic.
The night looks down upon us,
As in light you appear to me
Just as magical as you truly are–

Unveiling.

WHERE THE HEART
GOES TO BLOOM

I LONG FOR A GOLDEN SUNSET WITH YOU

You know my body now,
& I know yours.
We've placed so many lifetimes,
Within the layers of this love,
That your hands no longer find my waist,
& I no longer paint the sky,
With fingertips over your chest
Upon morning birdsong.

But the coffee still brews delicately
& somehow clocks skip ahead
With no spare time for the skin-to-skin,
Wait in the kitchen for that shared first-sip.

You leave & already,
I long for a golden sunset with you.
A feet-in-the-sand embrace,
On the everyday-ness of us.
For the way we always seem to come together again–
With as much wildfire as the first time
Has my breath caught in a place
Somewhere between my heart & the sky–

Cyclic love.

WHERE THE HEART
GOES TO BLOOM

Your song is one sung,
By the courageous & true.

WHERE THE HEART
GOES TO BLOOM

Forgetting your way is natural.

–start again.

WHERE THE HEART GOES TO BLOOM

I plant daisies with my imagination, as I walk the field at dusk. Do you feel the callings of *more* at the centre of your chest upon each dawn?

Today, I stopped my chasing, this frantic run from all that longs to crumble who I thought I had to be in this world.

Tomorrow, the sun will teach me over again to stop & turn toward all that is true & all that takes its own sweet, honey-soaked time.

WHERE THE HEART
GOES TO BLOOM

& my life is so much sweeter, because you exist.

WHERE THE HEART
GOES TO BLOOM

You are one of the most powerful dreams a dreamer can dream.

WHERE THE HEART
GOES TO BLOOM

May deep resounding breaths find you in whatever season you find yourself.

WHERE THE HEART
GOES TO BLOOM

True contentment—the aftermath of quiet treks through shadowed terrain & midnight tears.

WHERE THE HEART GOES TO BLOOM

A steady undercurrent,
A subtle pulse—

The love we share so well.

Much has been written, forged, birthed from the endless depths of you. You are the sacred stories to be told of what lies within the shadows. A mirror, to all that is unseeable. But felt—like nothing ever felt before.

WHERE THE HEART
GOES TO BLOOM

If you ever feel you need to go, I will send you brightly on your way with what we've so tenderly grown.

WHERE THE HEART
GOES TO BLOOM

Sun-beams, bright lights, afternoon kisses—I am home again. Home again—in birdsong outside my window. Home again—softening into his chest, beating with roses to bloom. Telling old stories of alleyway nights smoking cigarettes as the rain fell on our heads, as the band played your favourite reggae tune. Home again—in the simple bliss between fresh linen sheets. Home again—in cutting the roses off the backyard trees to spread beauty & learn of impermanence. Home again—in cold black coffee as I got my heart caught up in a dream that truly took me somewhere.

Home again—whenever I choose to be.

WHERE THE HEART
GOES TO BLOOM

It's strange that the things that we run from, are often the places where completeness could come from.

WHERE THE HEART
GOES TO BLOOM

We got lost in the what & why
Breathing magic into our dreams
Trusting the growing pains
Were only expanding us.

Whilst the great divine
Worked bit by bit
Layer by layer
On the how & when.

VELVET PINK

Delicate velvet pink
& wine stained red—
You showed me
Love could be open,
Stable, yet gentle
Like cherry blossoms
Greeting the midday sun,
That still close
To borrow further
Deep into the night.

Planting roots further
Into the earth
Into our breath
& the marrow
In our bones
That our love
Grew dancingly upon.

WHERE THE HEART
GOES TO BLOOM

Curled up interlaced
Together in sweet darkness.
Your hand traces
The uneven line
My spine writes,
Beneath my breasts.

The centre you hold
Like the oldest tree
In a windstorm
Nurturing, strong.

& when you trace
Your hands over me
You trace art
Of unseen magic
& mysteries that move
The earth on her axis–

& boy she ever moves.

AFTER WE GO

'Busy' hours tick by
& behind days' soundtrack
Behind month's album
Behind years' fast forward—

Lay a white noise
An electrifying undercurrent
That makes my eyes swell
With oceans & heavy rain—
Loves expression.

That stops everything.
Dust stops its float in mid-
Airborne fire
In the pit of my stomach.

& it's you—
Your skin on mine,
Those lines between eyebrows
When in deep trance &
Perseverance through

WHERE THE HEART
GOES TO BLOOM

A falling of each day,
Spent on the clock
Rather than wrapped up,
With time on pause.

Rain falling cheeks,
With pure surrender
To each other
In a delight in

All the magic
That is exploding
Unapologetically–
Those blue eyes.

Eyes that hold me
When lost in mine,
More than strong arms
Of anyone who has ever
Attempted to hold
The weight of
Who I truly am.

WHERE THE HEART GOES TO BLOOM

Eyes that remind me,
Love isn't measurable
Within linear boxed-in
Confinements of
Graspable time & reality.

Eyes that whisper a truth
That a sacred love
Like the one we hold
Is an invitation
Into all that is timeless–
Into an eternity that exists
Within each one of us.

The one that was here
Before we ever were.
& the one that will remain
Long after we go.

Out of control–
All we can do is
Love harder,
Fall deeper,
Breathe longer breaths

& just be with it.

GRATITUDES

This book was birthed out of the generosity of many human hearts who have truly shown up for me–just as I am–within my creative journey. You have shown me the patience, grace & love a soul can only long & hope to experience within its lifetime. I have found myself in a deep transformative metamorphosis, wrapped up within a collective one. & what I have learnt is that the struggle is not as necessary as I once thought it to be.

Through a gathering in the kind of unconditional support from women I have never truly known until this point, I have found my way home. But not without the willingness to 'go there' to the deepest, darkest place of myself first. & to be willing to let it all go in an instant. I have started celebrating the ability to drop it all for a midday swim or nap, to not make anything more important than the callings of my own heart. Directioning my heart in this way has seen much unraveling, tears & newfound joys. It's almost as if I am finding myself in a new body, in a completely new reality from this 'lightening up.' Whatever happens within, cannot help but also happen without.

I have realised my fear of true deep connection is my own, this fear being the only thing that repeats the narrative & patterning of not feeling truly seen or heard. Enough of that. It's time to step up & lean into the cushioning support of community & drop stories that keep us in fear & hardness.

Thank you to YOU–the reader. I have heard that grief occurs when love has no place to go. You give me the a landing place for my love to flow. For that I can never thank you enough.

GRATITUDES

We are never alone in this journey, & I hope that the words within these pages have spoken to parts of your soul, held space for your wounds & helped mend the most tender parts of you. I can never thank you enough for picking up this book & finding a place for it within your heart & home. I couldn't be doing this work, without you.

To my little growing family, Matt & our love-filled fur children Sadie & Dallas, thank you for holding so much space for all of my depth, intensity & potency. It was a true jackpot, finding you–so unwaveringly loving as I constantly shed skin & soften into new ways of being. You have taught me the healing power in true reciprocity, having my deepest self reflected back & accepted graciously.

To the women who walk alongside me, who have taught me how to trust again, in the bigness of my own heart: Kate & family, Keelin, Phoebe, Tara, Emma, Sophie, Jane & so many more. I love to think that you all really truly know who you are. Thank you, thank you, thank you.

I dare you to discover the magic that is already there inside of you. You are powerful beyond measure. You do not need to be scared of what you are anymore.

I love you, I love you, I love you.

ABOUT THE AUTHOR

Jessi Simpson is the multi-disciplinary creative behind Bloompress: an integration of poetry & brand creation, intuition & photography.

Jessi helps others to transform their experiences into medicine for the world. Capturing what is real, Jessi shows others that they too, can be more than one thing in this world, that the heart desires for much more than we have been led to believe is possible.

Jessi first published 'love & cigarettes' in 2018, in a season of deep questioning, heartbreak & intensity. This current work has been in the creative pipeline for over a year & it wasn't until Jessi realised that it needed to be a re-creation of the original work that it started to effortlessly write itself.

Through all Jessi does—whether it's shooting a brand session, creating yoga & astrology tools, or mentoring like-minds, all springs from the same deep intention: to heal the relationship to our body, our community, our creativity & our world. Her work is deeply informed by metaphysics, spiritual practice & every day unfolding.

Jessi now resides in a place where the mountains kiss the sea, tucked away in an old 1970s beach (love) shack with her lover & dogs in the Mid North Coast of New South Wales. Her days are spent slowly with yoga & coffee in the mornings, followed by simple days full of work that sets her alight.

You can also find Jessi's work featured within Slow Journal, Wellbeing Wild Magazine, Destination Magazine, Small Collective Magazine & Eye of Horus Cosmetics.

www.ingramcontent.com/pod-product-compliance
Lightning Source LLC
Chambersburg PA
CBHW062026290426
44108CB00025B/2796